2☹2☺

LIFE IN THE EYE OF A STORM

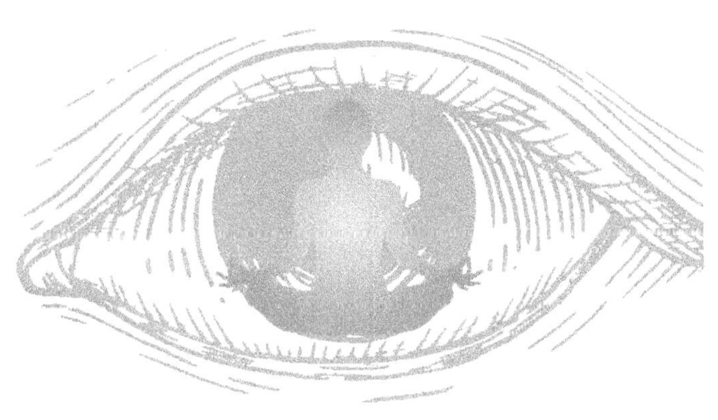

Dr. Vinay Bansal

CONTENTS

The ongoing storm will change the world forever in the same way the two world wars have changed it. The global power balance will change once again. Some nations will lose power. Some will emerge as new powers.

If you still think it is less than a world war, then let me tell you, trains were never stopped even during the war. Never were all international and domestic flights cancelled. In this digital era, caller tunes had never been changed by the governments. There was never a mass lockdown affecting almost the entire world. In fact, only a limited number of nations were mainly affected by those catastrophic wars.

It will be affecting almost all spheres of our life for a long time. Businesses will never be the same. The patterns of human interactions may change.

Only the person who knows how to remain in the eye of the storm will win. All others will be destroyed by its fierceness.

We were not taught in schools to tackle such situations. This is a new challenge. There are hundreds and thousands of suggestions. We don't know which path to follow.

In Hindu mythology, Arjun's son learnt the method of breaking the Chakravyuh (labyrinth) inside the womb. Similarly, at the earliest, we have to learn and understand the importance of breaking the labyrinth of negative thoughts and attitudes.

This book will take various aspects ranging from physical well-being to mental well-being. It will help you discover the path to your inner peace. It will deliver you a new space, inside you, which is never affected by external storms, just like the eye of a storm that remains calm in the midst of raging adversity.

Challenges for Mental Balance

You must have heard about mental conditions like depression, anxiety, addiction etc. increasing in the past few decades. The trends of these conditions have been seen to be more prevalent in nuclear families. It is also seen that high-income families face the strain of loneliness more often since the ability to travel and live in faraway places increases the distance among family members.

Incidence of mental illnesses is inversely related to human interactions. Generations of our forefathers were living closely, dependent on each other. There were a lot of human interactions and that helped in the leakage of built emotions. Due to such close interactions, intense emotions had a positive escape.

On the other hand, nowadays more and more human interactions are being replaced with digital communications, especially in the present situations. Digital interactions are directly proportional to mental diseases. You may be wondering how physical interactions are inversely proportional and how digital interactions are directly proportional to the incidence of mental diseases. Allow me to explain-

Digital interactions may contain emoticons to express your feelings, but ask yourself, how many times have you really 'laughed out loud' while writing LOL. In most cases, the emotions we feel are very different from the emoticons we use.

The human mind and brain are better suited for one task at a time. Multitasking is just a myth. In fact, while multitasking, we are continuously shifting our focus from one task to the next. In digital interactions, at the same time, we tend to interact with multiple people. We use different social media platforms - WhatsApp, Instagram, Telegram, Twitter, Facebook and the list goes on. In each app, we tend to see multiple messages. These multiple messages with multiple angles of thoughts confuse and burden our mind. With more and more digital interactions, we are burdened, stressed and become irritated.

The following chapters will take you through a journey that will make you aware of what are the most important things in life. It will help you find peace in this digital era that is a storm for the mind.

In the following chapters, we will start with some very basic questions of life and will try to find the answers.

What can be the most basic question about life?

Chapter 1 - What is a Perfect Life?

What are the parameters to decide if a life is perfect?

Most societies perceive a perfect life as a life with a lot of money, prosperity, reputation and success in different walks of life. They perceive a perfect life as life like that of Donald Trump, Bill Gates, Sachin Tendulkar and all the big names in the world. You must have seen some very successful people, who are very prosperous and even at the top of their career but still are not living a happy life. Their life is far from perfect. We hear about family disputes of celebrities, drug addiction and even suicides by the people who are at the top of the success ladder.

Does that mean the perfect life is not the same as material success?

Yes, the perfect life is not only equal to material success. A person should be stable physically, emotionally and spiritually, as well. Nowadays, we keep running after material pleasures so much that we forget to take care of our biggest wealth- our body, mind and soul. The perfect life is a balance of material success, health, mind, soul, family relations and social relations.

But, how do you balance all these? What will be our guiding light?

For this, we need to first understand the actual purpose of life. We need to understand the tools and techniques that will help us to get and keep this state of life. In the following chapters, we will learn these concepts.

Chapter 2 - What is the purpose of life?

Let's consider this scenario-

There is a bus which is designated to travel around the most beautiful city ever created and its only purpose is to show the visitors the beauty of this city. It has ten stops and people hop on and off at different stops. Here the trick is that only the driver decides which passengers will board or deboard, and in which instance. Passengers even receive small packets of food and drink during their travel. People enjoy their bus ride, even if they have to keep standing. They share food and drinks with all co-passengers who don't have enough of it. And they have the most beautiful scenery to keep them company. When the time comes, they happily deboard at the station wherever the driver asks them.

But time makes you forget everything, even if it is the actual purpose of the journey. With time, we get used to doing things in an automatic, monotonous way. The same happened for this bus ride.

Wherein, some passengers forget the actual purpose of this ride. Instead of looking out of the window for the beautiful views, they keep competing with their co-passengers for the food and seats. They think other people, who are ahead of them in seating order, have a better view of the scenery outside. So, they constantly try to get to a seat ahead of them. In this competition, they forget the actual purpose of this ride. They are unhappy because they think they don't have the best seat. Even the person who is perceived to have the best seat can't enjoy his view in the fear of someone else replacing him. People keep collecting more and more food, much more than they need. They forget the needs of others in their selfish desire to get everything for themselves even if they have to get down at the last station, empty-handed. As passengers forget their actual purpose, they continue wasting their energy on trivial things that are not important at all.

Similar is our condition these days. We have forgotten that life is like a bus journey where we have to enjoy nature (created by the creator). We should share everything with our co-passengers to keep this ride smooth and enjoyable for all. But instead, we have entered into this unhealthy competition with them and it keeps us tense and unhappy all the time. Although, there may be nothing wrong in getting a better seat and having enough food, yet while getting these we shouldn't forget that the ultimate aim is to enjoy the ride. We don't know when the driver will pull the chain and ask us to deboard. And when that time arrives, we will have to leave all our seats and foodstuff here and board down leaving behind all the co-passengers and everything we once treasured.

- REMEMBER death is the best invention of (and inspiration for) life.

- One good way to remember the importance of life and of *today* is to get up in the morning and think/assume that this is the last day of our life. It will allow you to focus on the most important things in your life- your inner self and your relations. You'll get rid of the unnecessary burden of future planning. Remember, during the bus journey, the most important decisions are being made by the driver, so why worry? Just relax.

Chapter 3 - Unburden Yourself

While riding this bus of life, some people take the unnecessary burden about the journey of the bus. They keep thinking about the next station. *Will it be beautiful or not?*

They forget that they are not in charge of this bus. They unnecessarily burden themselves with future thoughts that are absolutely beyond their control. They forget that this bus has been running perfectly for ages, and their role is only to enjoy this ride. This unnecessary burden keeps them away from having the true pleasure of this amazing journey.

For example, in our body, the most important systems are blood circulation and breathing. While drowning or during a heart attack, we all have noticed that one can't survive for even a few minutes without these two systems. But see how nature has kept these important systems under the autonomous nervous system. They keep running even when we are asleep or busy throughout the day.

Same is with the Sun, the most important source of energy for the Earth. It rises and sets with its routine maintaining the perfect heat ratio necessary for life, without any human intervention. We need not worry about it. The same goes for the water cycle and nutrient cycles. Nature is running all these cycles perfectly.

We have a very limited role in these most important things. Nature is like a parent making all the important decisions on behalf of a newborn child. Even decisions about our birth, family, economic and social status and our death are taken by nature. But some people keep on worrying about whether they are making proper decisions or not. Rather we should unburden ourselves and enjoy this ride as a neonate enjoys in the lap of her mother. Let nature do its job. After all, it has been doing it even before we existed.

However, we need to do some little things to make this ride more beautiful for us and our fellow passengers. The most essential thing here is to clean the glasses that we are wearing. These glasses, if dirty, make the whole scene dirty. By glasses, I mean the ***attitude*** towards life. This attitude decides our happiness, peace, success, relationships, goals and achievements. So, the need is to see everything through a positive angle.

That change of attitude will come from further changing your thinking patterns that we will discuss in detail, in the coming chapters.

Chapter 4 - Fill your tank first

Once a tribal head from the desert areas of Africa visited a well-developed Western city. It was the first time that any of his primitive tribe had travelled outside their native area to see a developed city. He was fascinated to see the development. But one thing that fascinated him the most was that there were taps that you could open and water flows. He had never imagined such a thing. In his tribe, bringing water from a distant source was one of the main challenges of life.

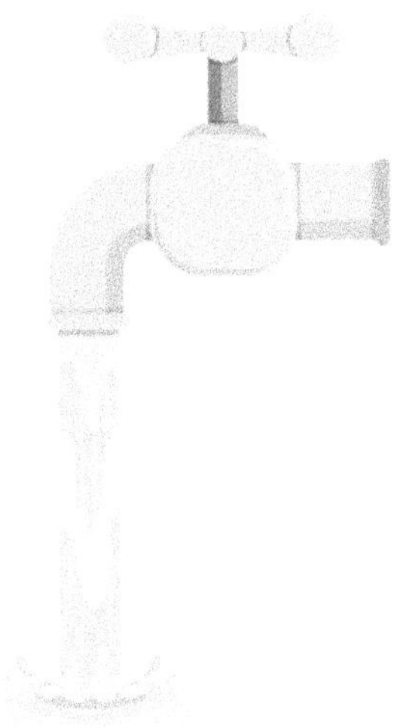

When he came back, from the city to his tribe, he called all his fellow tribesmen. He declared that he will show them a wonderful thing that they would have never imagined even in their wildest dreams. All the tribesmen became excited. He opened his bag and carefully picked up a piece of tap that he had purchased from the city. He told his tribesmen that he can make the water flow from this tiny object. He carefully kept an empty bucket below the tap and slowly opened the tap. All the present tribesmen were excited to see the flow of water. But to their disappointment, no water flowed out. The head was very surprised as to why the water was not flowing here, while it was flowing in the city.

He did not understand the concept that it was not only the tap but also the pipelines and the tank that was causing the availability of water. He merely saw the outer part of the water system but did not understand the mechanism behind this flow.

The same is the case with most of us. We see the flow of energy, positivity, happiness and success in successful people. We try to imitate their routine and lifestyle superficially. But we do not realise that the actual source of their energy and motivation is somewhere else. There is a pipeline of positive attitudes, beliefs and habits. There is a storage tank in the form of the subconscious mind, that is connected to a further source of water that is infinite intelligence. We all already have the infrastructure of this pipeline and tank. The only need is to find it and to tighten the connections so that the divine water can flow into our taps, as well.

Chapter 5 - Lifestyle

We all hear about lifestyle diseases these days- High BP (hypertension), diabetes, insomnia, anxiety and so on. These diseases are increasing thanks to our ever-changing lifestyle. But to stop them, we can't go to the primitive livelihood that was followed by our ancestors. We are in a different world, which is connected by technology and has its own set of different challenges and expectations.

So, the challenge is to live in the same environment, same family and friends' circle and still keep ourselves immune from the negatives of this lifestyle.

As we go on, we will discuss the most important routines that you can do anywhere and anytime, that will make you unsusceptible to these ill effects. You will audit and improve your performance just by remembering the same word 'LIFESTYLE'. We will expand this word and assign a particular body part, from head to toe, to each habit.

The first and most important is **LIFE.**

Remember what life is. What is the ultimate goal? *Remember the bus journey?* Live life from one day to the next.

It is like a cricket match. Take one ball at a time, put your heart and soul into that one single shot. You can't win a match if you keep thinking about the next ball or even the next over. Focus on each ball at a time. A week is like an over. Even if some balls don't go according to you, you still can cover up by playing better in the next balls. 50 overs are like 52 weeks a year. There will be Yorkers and bouncers of hard times. But you have to save your wicket of happiness by being patient and by sticking to your basics.

But remember, it is only a game. Don't take it too seriously. Play with full enthusiasm but don't forget, there is an organizer of this game who will take care of you even if you don't perform well. Unburdening yourself from the pressure of performance is the only key to success and enjoyment in this game.

The **key organ** in your body is **your head**. To relax, massage your head/forehead/eyebrows at regular intervals and think about life. Introspect your life but do not overdo it. Physical stimulation will relax your brain and will further help you think more positively and fruitfully.

S - SMILE

How many animals have you seen smiling? Smiling is a privilege that is given only to humans. Whenever you smile, on the physical side your face muscles relax. But on a bigger result, positive hormones are secreted in your body that produces a sensation of well-being and happiness.

Does it cost anything? Can't you smile at all the people and family members whom you meet every day? It will create positive vibes in your relationships. It will unburden you from tensions and worries.

Smiling is not only for cameras, but it is also for the mirror. Give yourself a big smile. After all, who is the most important person in your life? You. Yourself. If you are not happy, your relationships or your business can never be healthy. So, every morning when you wake up, give yourself a big hug and a big smile.

Some people, who don't smile often, find it difficult to do so. The key is - Fake it until you make it. After a few days of a fake smile, you'll get a beautifully natural smile adorning your face. This smile is contagious, more than anything else. It will lighten up your personal life, relationships and your business. Why not try it? Give a smile to everyone around you and if you are alone, find a mirror or at least the front camera of your phone

Here, the **key organ** is your face- **A face with a beautiful smile**. Smile while doing any work; you don't need the presence of any person or any reason to smile. Smiling is your natural state, so do so as often as you can.

T - THOUGHTS

Why do some people see the opportunity in some situations while others feel hopeless? Why the same weather is felt as pleasant by some and annoying by others. It all depends on our thoughts. The kinds of thoughts in a situation are influenced by our experiences, our belief systems and our circumstances.

Thoughts are like a child. They keep wandering between the past and the future. It is like a child who keeps sneaking in here and there when no one is watching her. But as soon as her mother arrives, she behaves normally. It is because the child knows what is good and what is bad. The only thing here is the need for continuous external observation. Similarly, we have to observe and control our thoughts.

Whenever you do this ritual, just see where your thoughts are wandering. They will align themselves just by this observation. Respect all your decisions of the past and be hopeful about the future. Both these things are out of your control. So, the simple sign here is folded hands; as if you are leaving this to the universal intelligence to decide. It will again unburden yourself and help clear your mind.

Sign- Folded hands. Observe your thoughts and join both your hands. This will put an end to the cascade of thoughts running through your mind. You will immediately feel a sense of relaxation and peace.

Y - YES

Why at times, we don't do the things we want to do? Like going to the gym, starting a new project or simply saying sorry! We keep lingering on these things without any sense or reason.

The cause may be lethargy in simple terms or inertia in scientific terms. Inertia is a natural law derived from Newton's first law. It says that the materials at rest remain at rest and materials in motion remain moving unless some external force is applied. The same logic applies to humans. Unless we are pressurised by our boss or circumstances, we tend to delay the good deeds in our life.

Our time on this beautiful earth is limited. And we don't know when our last station will come. It is a fact that at the end of your life, you only feel bad about the things you wanted to do, but didn't do. You rarely feel bad about the things you did incorrectly. I am not advising about starting any new adventure without proper preparation. I only say that if you want to do anything good for your family, this universe or for yourself, start today. Don't wait for the perfect time to come. Things will settle in place by themselves. As it is said- *if you want anything from the bottom of your heart, the whole universe strives to accomplish it.*

Sign- Kundli

Area - below the umbilicus and above the genital area.

It is an area where most of our hidden energy is present. We can tap or activate this energy by saying 'hmm...' loudly. This sound will strike at the area below the umbilicus, that is the Kundli area. If you repeatedly say 'hmm...' 20-25 times, you will feel the energy inside you. So, whenever you are doing this ritual, say 'hmm...' and take your thoughts to this area and analyse what are the things you are putting off until tomorrow. Do these now, because 'now' is always the best time to accomplish anything you desire.

L - LIBERATE

How many addictions do you have? Addiction means the things/habits that you continue with no useful result or rather harmful results. Addiction may include several things but the most important addiction of our generation is 'screen addiction'. It is the addiction that is affecting all age groups, genders, social strata and geographical areas.

Albert Einstein had aptly said- *"I fear the day that technology will surpass our human interaction. The world will have a generation of idiots."* That day has arrived. With artificial intelligence and the use of the same in social media, addiction is further increasing. Nowadays, your mobile/laptop knows what your interests are. It shows you the links of entertainment videos or shopping websites that are hard to ignore. It is like technology is making us decide what we will see next, what we need to pursue next. This addiction is affecting our relationships and our peaceful existence. It takes us away from the beauty of nature and our vast intelligence.

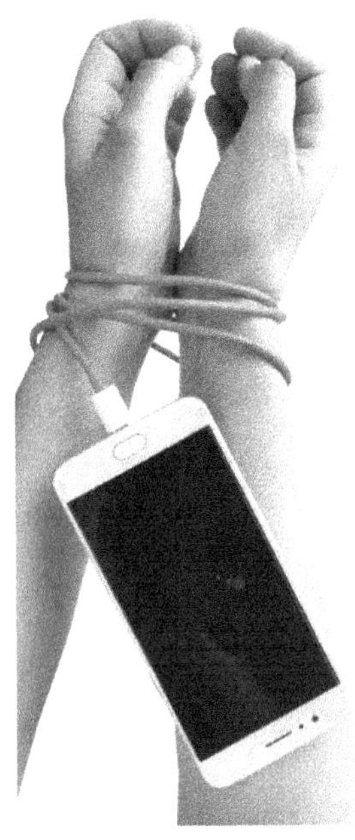

People are now constantly checking Facebook status, WhatsApp stories, Instagram pics, or tens of other notifications that pop up on the screen. These stories and pictures create a virtual reality that is far away from the actuality. People, while posting on social media, artificially act as if they are much happier and enjoying their life to the fullest. In reality, they may suffer from depression or strained relationships. But on social media, they behave like everything is perfect. Thus, creating a false sense of desire in the viewers. In the same way, some people exaggerate their suffering on social media.

Social media is a mechanical way to express human feelings, that gives little pleasure or relief to the person sharing these posts. But it creates jealousy, competition and a sense of envy in the minds of the viewers. The viewers want to achieve the same happiness as shared by the person who posted these pictures/videos/posts. This creates a source of unhappiness for all users.

We need to *liberate* ourselves from this addiction. Otherwise, this invention of man will consume our mind and brain. We need to get away from this unnecessary and unhealthy stuff on social media.

Sign- The signs of liberation are **in your pockets**. Whenever you do this ritual, just put your mobile on aero-plane mode and keep it in your pocket. If there are no pockets in your trousers, then you can put it in your bag; anything that will help divert your mind from the false lure of social media.

E - EXERCISE

Exercise is a great way of keeping your body active to its full potential. It energizes your body parts. It produces certain neurotransmitters that generate a good feeling in our brain.

You should maintain a routine of exercise. Half an hour of exercise for five days a week is good for your heart and your mind. This exercise may include jogging, running, yoga, gym workout, treadmill or any other active sport. Just walking will not be included in this definition. Exercise should be such that it produces sweat and increases your heartbeat and respiratory rate.

Even during your working hours, you should take a break and activate all your joints. All possible movements for the joints are very relaxing and also good for mind relaxation. Start with your toes. Flex and extend your toes. Stretch your legs and if possible, try a few simple leg-stretches. These exercises will ensure that the uneasiness acquired in your body, by sitting at a place for hours, is removed.

Sign- The sign of exercise is **your legs**. As legs are an important part of any exercise, so while doing this ritual, a thought on legs will make you aware of the exercise that your body and mind needs.

Chapter 6 – C2A Meditation

This section requires your active participation

C2A Meditation is a scientific technique of meditation developed by combining the vast knowledge of Yoga, ancient meditations and research works of renowned psychologists, especially Mr. Jose Silva. It completely relaxes your mind and increases your efficiency multifold. It is very easy to learn and follow. You can do it in any clothes and on any furniture. It is even possible to do it during working hours as well. It is based on classical conditioning of the mind, that enables you to perform this meditation in a very short time when you become used to it. After 1-2 weeks of practice, you can further achieve the higher and deeper level of this meditation for your professional growth; be it a better team leader, a confident speaker or a better decision-maker.

This mediation is to be done with eyes closed. You can't do it while driving or during any activity that involves the use of your senses. A mild headache may occur if you are doing it for the first time, but it passes away after 4-5 cycles of meditation. Here are some steps involved in this C2A Meditation:

We'll first discuss the science behind all these steps and then learn it step by step-

1. Switch off your phone and any other source that can disturb you for the next 20-30 minutes. It is a much-needed step, otherwise, these distractions will hamper the peace and silence that you will achieve during this Meditation.

2. Clear your surroundings and sit in such a manner that your body is in minimum contact with your surroundings. Do two rounds of 'Bhastrika', that will involve the movement of your arms up and down. It would be better if you had enough space around you. Pay attention to your breath. Observe how the air is entering and leaving your nostrils. Breath in and out slowly.

3. Close your eyes and start Bhastrika, again. This posture involves the movement of your arms with your breath. Forcefully breathe in and move your arms above your head. While breathing in, your elbows should be straight and fingers open as shown in the picture. While exhaling, fist your hands and bring them near your shoulders.

INHALE – Raise Your Hands Up

EXHALE – Bring your Hands down

Do two rounds of Bhastrika. In the first round, while exhaling, do the count with English alphabet- A to Z. In the second round, count in reverse from 26 to 1. After each round, relax your hands on your thighs and focus on your breathing. After each round, you will feel new energy coursing through your body. Observe the flow of that energy throughout your body.

Bhastrika will remove all your lethargy. It will make you more alert. The effect of these two rounds will be equal to a cup of strong coffee. You can do these rounds separately also, whenever you feel like having coffee.

Bhastrika will remove all your lethargy. It will make you more alert. The effect of these two rounds will be equal to a cup of strong coffee. You can do these rounds separately also, whenever you feel like having coffee.

1. Once relaxed, contract and squeeze all your body muscles. Start with the forehead. Then you have to squeeze your eyelids, then clench your teeth. Make a tight fist with your hands. Squeeze your toes. Apply full pressure for 5 seconds.

   Then, relax all your muscles starting from the forehead and following the same sequence. Relax for 5 seconds.

   Do 3 rounds of it. It will increase your awareness of all tissues. It will increase the blood flow to your body parts. It will further help you in going deeper into the next rounds.

2. This step involves rolling your eyeballs while keeping your eyes closed. It is as if you are looking at an object 30 degrees above the level of your eyes. This position of eyeballs is the position of meditation.

3. With your eyes remaining closed, roll your eyes at a 30-degree angle upwards, and form a figure of a white coloured capital letter 'C' three times.

4. Now when on level C, relax your body by relaxing the muscles of the head, the forehead, the eyes, face, throat, then the shoulders, the upper arms, the elbow and arms, hands, chest, abdomen, thighs, and finally your leg muscles and toes.

Feel that your feet and legs don't belong to your body, then your thighs, chest, hands, elbow and shoulders do not belong to your body.

This is **level C**, level of full-body relaxation.

5. Again, with your eyes closed, roll your eyes up at 30 degrees and visualise white coloured capital letter 'B' three times.

   You are at **level B**, which is full mental relaxation. Give instructions to your mind that no outer sounds should distract you. Your thoughts will come and go but will not stay in your mind. You are fully mentally relaxed at this level. You control your thoughts.

6. Again, roll your eyes upwards at 30-degree angle and visualise white coloured capital letter 'A' three times.

   You are at **level A**, and you will visualise yourself travelling to a beautiful cloud. This cloud is much above Earth and you will separate from it. Earth is moving, but this cloud is standing still. Feel the cool breeze touching your skin. Breathe in deeply. This breeze brings positivity, joy, energy, enthusiasm, hope and confidence inside you.

   Now, count from 100 to 1 and go deeper at this level. Wait for around 1 minute. At this moment, 1 minute is equal to a 1-hour of deep sleep.

7. Count from 1 to 5 and slowly come out of this deep level. While coming out, give yourself instructions that after opening your eyes you will be fully awake and will feel better than before. Assure yourself of a brighter time to come.

8. Rub your palms and place them over your eyes. Open your eyes slowly.

   Feel the difference and enjoy your day.

THE WAY AHEAD

As the eye of a storm remains calm amidst the chaos on the outside, this book has been written to provide the readers with the right mindset and techniques to achieve calmness during these restless times.

As we already see in the news every day about the pain and the suffering, this book is meant to serve as a diversion. This book wasn't meant to give facts that can be found everywhere but about attaining calmness in these restless times.

The knowledge penned down in these few pages will serve as the correct operating system for our body. Utilise this time to upgrade your operating systems for inner peace. With time, many viruses may keep attacking your operating system to decrease its efficiency. C2A meditation will act as an antivirus for you to keep your operating system, of inner peace, intact. You only need to scan your system once a day through C2A meditation.

In the end, I want to thank all my family members and all my friends for helping with this book. A special thanks to Dr. Khushboo, Dr. Parlad Garg, Dr. Deepty Bansal, Dr. Rakesh Garg,

Mr. Suraj Kumar and Dr. Khushpreet Kaur for their valuable suggestions and Ms. Shruti Dutta Banik for editing. A special thanks to Google images, Artplusmarketing, 4570book and Sociview for providing very apt images to put forward our points in an effective manner.

Last but not the least, a special thanks to all the readers from the core of my heart. Without readers, a book has no value. I hope you all enjoyed the book and I hope these few pages will help to make your coming life more peaceful and meaningful.

If you need any further assistance in the form of recorded C2A meditation audio or any other advice, feel free to contact me at dr.vinaybansal@gmail.com or by WhatsApp at +91 98727 73450. Your suggestions for improvement of this book are always welcome.

The storm will pass but as long as it is here, we will be its centre. We will embody its calmness.

With heartfelt regards, and a prayer for your safety,

Dr. Vinay Bansal

NOTES

NOTES

NOTES

NOTES

www.ingramcontent.com/pod-product-compliance
Ingram Content Group UK Ltd.
Pitfield, Milton Keynes, MK11 3LW, UK
UKHW021644190726
13853UKWH00001B/41

9 798640 242218